Boodle and
Her Missionary Family

Boodle and
Her Missionary Family

by Amy Sherrard

Edited by Rachel Nelson
Illustrated by Ruthie Reeves
(granddaughters)

My Bible First

Boodle and Her Missionary Family
by Amy Sherrard (1917–2022)

ISBN: 9781092460347

Dedicated to

boys and girls who love animals
and are kind to them.

Contents

Elwood and Amy Sherrard
June 4, 1944

Forward

Little girls don't stay little very long, and Little Amy didn't stay little, either. She grew and grew until she was five foot two. Well, that is not very tall, but Little Amy never worried about being tall because she made up for it with her sparkling personality, abundant ideas, and seemingly endless energy to make them happen!

When she was all grown up she went to college and became a nurse. Best of all, Little Amy married a tall, handsome, wonderful man named Elwood whom she met in college. A few years later, they had their own little girls, Dena and Sherry.

It wasn't long before Little Amy and Tall Elwood began to dream about being missionaries. One day in 1952 the little family of four boarded a big ship sailing for Singapore. They waved and waved big white handkerchiefs to Little Amy's parents standing on the wharf. There were some tears in those big handkerchiefs because they knew they would not see their loved ones again for five long years. But oh, what exciting things awaited them in Singapore, and six years later in the Philippines! There were so many strange sights, sounds, and smells.

In this book you will meet their favorite pets. Boodle came as a cuddly black puppy. Would Smoky, the Siamese cat, get along with Boodle? There were Flip, Flop, Flash, and Dash, but they were just goldfish and couldn't do tricks, so you won't hear about them. But watch out for little Darling, the saucy parakeet! She nearly flies off the pages of the book as she dives into so much trouble you will wonder how she comes out alive. And finally there is Spooky, the black cat that nobody ever forgot once they met her. So let's get started with *Boodle and Her Missionary Family*.

—Dena Guthrie, daughter

Boodle Joins the Family

Boodle. What a funny name for a puppy! Six-year-old Dena and little four-year-old Sherry laughed as they watched the tiny black puppy racing around the yard of their home in Singapore. She was happily sniffing and checking out every little corner.

Mommy, and especially Daddy, were enjoying the new puppy, too. Daddy was remembering that when he was a little boy, the name of his favorite dog was Boodle, too.

"How come you called your doggie Boodle, Daddy?" Dena wanted to know.

Daddy thought a few seconds and then shook his head. "I don't know how he got his name; it just seemed like the right name, I guess."

"But your Boodle was a he, and our Boodle is a she. Does that matter?" Sherry wanted to know.

"I don't think it matters," Daddy laughed. "Let's see if she cares. "Here Boodle, Boodle, Boodle," he called. And Boodle came racing across the lawn, her silky black ears flopping up and down as she ran to him.

"Smart puppy. You already know your name." Mommy smiled as she picked up the puppy and snuggled her face against the soft fur, while Boodle wiggled and tried to give her happy, wet, doggie kisses.

Before going into the house, Mommy reminded the family that there were some things to remember. Boodle was still a little puppy, and this was the first time she had been away from her mommy. At first, she would probably be lonesome for her brother and sister puppies and her

10

mommy. She would need lots of love.

Mommy also said that they must always remember to never ever spank Boodle with their hands. Their hands must always be gentle and kind. They must be careful about scolding her if she was naughty. Mommy said that animals learn by being praised, not scolded.

"How would you feel if I shouted at you and spanked you when you didn't even know why? Would you want to come the next time I called, or would you be scared?" Mommy asked.

Dena and Sherry looked sober. "We'd be scared," they both said.

"Of course you would," Mommy agreed. "I'll help you teach Boodle how to be happy and obedient, without being afraid of you," she promised.

Inside the house, everyone laughed at how funny Boodle looked as she slipped and skidded and tumbled on the slippery tile floor. Boodle thought it was fun, too. Her little tail wagged, and she barked as she slid around every time she tried to run.

After Boodle and the family had supper and worship, it was bedtime for Dena and Sherry. Mommy had put a newspaper in one corner of the bathroom. "Boodle will soon learn to always use the newspaper when she needs to," she explained. "When she gets older, she'll let us know when she needs to go outside."

The girls put a soft towel close to the newspaper for Boodle to sleep on. And they stayed with the tired little puppy until she was sound asleep. Then the girls quietly closed the bathroom door and went to bed, too.

The house was very quiet. But not for very long.

Boodle Learns to Obey

Boodle was sound asleep in the bathroom. Then, suddenly, she woke up. The bathroom was dark, and she was all alone. She had never been alone before, and she didn't like it at all.

She sat up and opened her little mouth; and oh, the sad wailing sounds that came out! They were enough to break anyone's heart. But they were also loud enough to wake up all the neighbors.

Mommy got up, quickly folded a newspaper, and hurried to the bathroom. When she opened the door, she could hardly see the sad little black puppy in the dark room. Boodle stopped crying at once and started whining happily. But instead of petting her, Mommy gave the puppy a little swat with the newspaper. Boodle yipped as if Mommy had hit her hard. "No, Boodle," Mommy said in a firm voice, and then she quickly closed the door.

Boodle was quiet for a few seconds. She was probably trying to figure out what had happened. Then she started loudly crying again.

Quickly Mommy opened the door and did exactly what she had done the first time. After she closed the door, Boodle waited longer before crying. But as soon as she started, Mommy did exactly the same thing again. After that, Boodle was quiet for a long time, while Mommy waited. Then the crying started again; but when the puppy heard Mommy coming, she stopped at once. And she didn't start again. She didn't want another spanking.

Of course, the whole family petted and praised the

darling puppy the next morning.

After that first obedience lesson, smart little Boodle was always quiet at night. And all anyone had to do when Boodle did something naughty, was to pick up a paper, and say firmly, "No, Boodle," and Boodle knew just what that meant. Her ears would go down, her fluffy tail would go between her legs, and her eyes would look, oh, so sad.

"Good doggie," someone would say, and right away she was back to her happy little self again.

One day, one of the neighbors came by to see the new puppy. "Aren't you going to cut off Boodle's tail?" she asked. Dena's and Sherry's eyes grew wide. Cut off Boodle's tail? They had never even thought of such a thing.

"Why would we cut off Boodle's tail?" Dena wanted to know. "Aren't dogs supposed to have tails? Isn't that how God made dogs?"

"Well," the neighbor explained, "Boodle is mostly cocker spaniel. See her long, soft ears and the long hair starting to grow on her legs? Most owners of cocker spaniels take their dogs to a vet for surgery to cut off their tails while they are still little puppies."

Dena and Sherry couldn't stand the thought of cutting off Boodle's lovely tail. "We want her to keep her tail," they told the neighbor. And that was that. Boodle got to keep her beautiful tail.

It seemed that Boodle's tail and ears and eyes could all talk. When she was happy, her ears tried to stand up. If she was standing, her tail waved back and forth like a flag; or if she was sitting down, it thumped on the floor. She even looked as if she were smiling.

Boodle Makes a New Friend

Boodle was growing fast, and the whole family loved her. Dena and her little sister Sherry never got tired of playing with her. And they loved to teach her tricks.

One day, a lady brought a large, beautiful Siamese cat to the house. She wanted Dena and Sherry to have the cat. Everyone knows that cats and dogs don't usually get along very well. As the girls held the cat, Boodle sat with her head cocked to one side and stared at it. The cat looked right back at Boodle as if to say, "I'm not one bit scared of you, black dog."

Boodle thumped her tail up and down on the floor as she kept staring at the cat. When the girls put the cat down, it kept looking at Boodle, and then it walked right over to her and purred loudly as it rubbed against Boodle. Boodle's tail thumped harder. Dena and Sherry smiled. Mommy smiled, too. And, of course, the cat got to stay.

The cat's thick fur was a soft, creamy white. His ears, tail, and paws were brown. His eyes were blue. He was beautiful, and he acted as if he had lived in their home all his life. It took a while to think of what to call him, but finally the family decided his name would be Smoky.

Smoky and Boodle became best friends right away, and how they loved playing together! Tag and hide and seek were probably their favorite games. Smoky could hide in all kinds of places that Boodle couldn't get to, and Smoky could do all kinds of things that Boodle couldn't do. But that didn't stop them from slipping and sliding on the floor as they chased each other from one end of the house to the other.

Like all cats, Smoky was clean—very, very clean. Boodle couldn't seem to understand why Smoky would sit and lick and lick himself and wash his face so many times every day. Every time Smoky ate food, or even took a drink of water, he always had to clean his face. Boodle would cock her head and watch Smoky, patiently waiting for him to finish. Sometimes she would bark at him as if to say, "Hurry up! Why are you taking so long? Come on! It's time to play!"

Smoky would finally get through. Then he would take time to stretch. When he got through with that, suddenly he would take off like a shot out of a gun, with Boodle right after him. Around and around they would go.

Smoky would run under chairs that were too low for Boodle to squeeze under. Or he would jump up onto something that was too high for Boodle to reach. Then Boodle would bark at Smoky as if to say, "That's not fair!" and Smoky would finally come out from under the chair, or hop down from his high perch so they could keep on playing.

One evening when they both got tired, the family watched something very funny happen.

Boodle Gets a Bath

When Boodle and Smoky both got tired of playing, Boodle would stretch out on the cool tile floor, and Smoky would curl up right against Boodle's warm tummy. Then they would both go to sleep.

One evening, Mommy, Daddy, and the girls were all reading; and Boodle and Smoky were both asleep. Pretty soon Smoky woke up. He sat up, looked down at Boodle, and decided that Boodle needed a bath. He walked around to Boodle's head and started to lick, and lick, and lick.

Boodle loved it, and kept very still. But after a while, Smoky stopped. He looked back and forth all the way from the tip of Boodle's nose down to the end of Boodle's tail.

Perhaps he was thinking, "This bath is going to take a long, long time. I don't think I'll ever be able to finish." But he kept on patiently licking and licking while the family laughed at what was happening.

Finally he looked all the way to Boodle's tail again. "I guess I'll stop," Smoky must have decided, because he stretched and walked off to find something else to do until Boodle woke up.

Boodle never did get a bath all over from Smoky, but she got plenty of face washings.

Another time, Boodle woke up first from her nap. She sat up and yawned. Then she looked down at Smoky and gently nudged him with her paw. Then she held up her paw and wiggled it over Smoky. Finally, she gave a little bark as if to say, "Come on, Smoky, it's time to wake up and play!" And away they went.

Smoky didn't live with the family very long. Boodle missed him after he left; but she still had lots of fun with Dena and Sherry. She always wanted to be with them wherever they went.

When another missionary family came to live on the compound, everyone was happy. The new family had three children. Now there were more than a dozen children, and they all loved Boodle.

The new family got a tiny white dog with soft, long fur and black eyes. Perhaps those black eyes led them to call their little dog Beedy. Right away, Boodle and Beedy were best friends, even though Boodle was much bigger than Beedy.

Whenever Boodle got a chance, she would rush down the little hill to Beedy's house so they could play together. When they got tired, Beedy would curl up beside Boodle and they would both take a nap. But whenever the girls or Mommy called, "Boodle!" she would come racing home at once with her tongue hanging out and a doggie smile on her face.

Mommy told Dena and Sherry that Boodle and her friends were good examples of how children should always get along together and obey as quickly as Boodle did.

Then something happened that worried everyone on the compound.

Boodle and Beedy

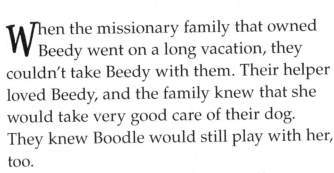

When the missionary family that owned Beedy went on a long vacation, they couldn't take Beedy with them. Their helper loved Beedy, and the family knew that she would take very good care of their dog. They knew Boodle would still play with her, too.

But one day while they were still away on that vacation, Beedy didn't want to play. She didn't want to eat, either. Of course the helper was very worried. She didn't know what to do; so she told the other missionaries, and they were worried, too. Even the doctor missionaries looked at Beedy and shook their heads. No one knew why she was sick.

Boodle was worried, too. She stayed right beside Beedy as much as she could. All the children on the compound were worried when she wouldn't even drink any water. No one wanted little Beedy to die. But no one knew what to do to help her. Even Boodle was sad. She would whine quietly and gently touch Beedy with her paw. But Beedy wouldn't even move, and she barely opened those shiny black eyes.

The missionaries were all praying about Beedy. But one of the missionary children got all the other children on the compound together. "Why don't we all hold hands in a circle around Beedy," she told them. "We can each pray to Jesus out loud, and ask Him to please make Beedy well again."

The children all thought that would be a wonderful idea, and they all went to where Beedy was lying. Poor Beedy was hardly breathing. The Chinese helper watched

18

the children as they held hands in a circle around Beedy. Boodle was there, too. Then the children all closed their eyes; and one by one, each of them prayed that Jesus would make Beedy well again.

When they finished praying, they opened their eyes and looked down at Beedy. They could hardly believe what they saw happening. Beedy opened those little black eyes, raised her shaggy head, looked around at all the children and at Boodle, and then got up and took a long drink of water.

"Jesus has healed Beedy! Jesus has healed Beedy!" the children shouted. They clapped their hands and rushed home to tell their parents. The helper was crying because she was so happy. Boodle's tail was wagging as she watched her little friend eating the good food that the helper brought.

That night every family on the compound thanked Jesus for doing such a wonderful miracle for little Beedy.

When Beedy's family got back from their vacation and learned about what had happened to their precious pet, they thanked everyone—especially the children—for caring so much about their little dog.

And you can be sure that their Buddhist Chinese helper never forgot that day and the amazing power of the God the missionaries worshiped. She probably told her friends about it. Do you think that might be one reason God let Beedy get sick?

Boodle Sneaks a Ride

"Daddy says some of the older students are going for a picnic at the beach today, and we can go, too," Mommy announced one morning after breakfast. "Would you like that?"

Daddy was the principal of a large mission school with hundreds of students from many places.

Dena and Sherry loved going to the beautiful, sandy beaches around the island of Singapore, so of course they wanted to go. Big palm trees waved their branches, sea gulls flew in the sky, and the food always tasted wonderful, even if a little sand got into it.

"May we take Boodle?" the girls asked.

"No, Boodle can't go this time," Mommy told them. "Our car will be crowded with students, and there really won't be room for her, so she'll have to stay home with our helper."

"Oh, Mommy," the girls begged, "Boodle loves the beach as much as we do. Can't we squeeze her in, somehow?" But Mommy stayed firm. "Not this time," she told them, and the girls knew there was no use begging. Begging was not allowed in their home.

When it was time to leave, everything was ready. Lunch was in the trunk along with swimming clothes, sun tan lotion, and all the other things that might be needed. Boodle was excited, but the girls had to say, "No, Boodle. You can't go this time."

Boodle looked sad as she slowly followed the car to pick up the girls from the school that would ride in the back seat. Dena and Sherry were in front with Mommy. There weren't rules in Singapore about seatbelts in those days, and the girls weren't very big anyway.

Mommy got out of the car for a few minutes. "Isn't Boodle going with us?" the other girls wanted to know. All the students loved Boodle, too. "Mommy said she can't come because there wouldn't be room," Dena told them.

Suddenly, the back door of the car opened and then closed again, and there were shuffling sounds in the back seat. Dena and Sherry looked around. The girls in the back seat put their fingers to their lips, "Shhh!" so Dena got onto her knees and peeked down to see what was happening.

She was sure she could see something under their legs, but it was too dark to be sure what it was. Soon Mommy got back into the car and they started off. "My, but it's very quiet in the back seat! Do you girls have enough room?" she asked.

"Oh, yes," they all answered together. "We have lots of room." And they chattered away all the rest of the trip.

At the beach, the car doors flew open, and guess who jumped out along with the laughing girls? Even Mommy had to laugh at Boodle.

What a wonderful time everyone had that day! And Boodle added a lot to the fun.

Boodle Gets Ready for Sabbath

Boodle never did understand Sabbath. After all, she was just a precious, innocent dog. But she was part of the family, and Dena and Sherry were determined that she always had to be ready for Sabbath along with the rest of the family.

"Boodle, it's time for your bath," they would announce every Friday afternoon. Boodle's tail and ears and head would go down, and she put her saddest look on her face, but she knew that bath time was a rule that never changed.

Dena and Sherry would put warm water in the side-by-side tubs. Her soap and her towels would be all ready. Then, they would pick her up and put her hind legs in one tub and her front legs in the other tub. They tried not to get any soap in her eyes, and Boodle would stand patiently while they scrubbed and rinsed her.

When they finally finished, they would lift Boodle out and say, "Shake, Boodle! Shake!" Boodle was glad to shake, and the girls would laugh as they watched her. Then they would do their best to dry her with towels and keep her inside the house.

Of course, Boodle would have to go out again before bedtime, and the girls could never understand why she would do her best to roll in something smelly before coming back. They always thought their perfumed soap made her smell nice.

When they got older, they learned that most dogs don't like the smell of perfume.

Boodle always knew when it was Sabbath morning. At

breakfast time, Boodle acted sad. She knew that everyone was going to be gone soon—even their helper—and she would be all alone. She would crawl under a stool in the kitchen with her head on the floor and just her nose and sad eyes showing.

Both Dena and Sherry had started to help with the kindergarten Sabbath school, and they took lots of pictures to show the children. Since the place where they helped teach was close by, they would come back to the house and leave everything except their Bibles before going back to church. When the girls came back after Sabbath school, Boodle wouldn't greet them. She knew they would be leaving again.

But when the family all got home after church, Boodle acted as if they had been gone for a week. She jumped and ran around as if she were going to burst with joy. She knew she would be with them the rest of the day.

When Boodle was fully grown, she was a big dog with silky, black hair. Her ears flapped like two wings when she ran, and her long beautiful tail wagged back and forth when she was happy.

Being big made it easy for Boodle to put her paws up on things and look around. But being able to do that got her into trouble one time.

Boodle Gets Caught

Mommy had told Dena and Sherry to never give food to Boodle when they were eating at the table, so Boodle never learned to beg like some dogs do. She loved to please people, and sometimes in the kitchen Dena or Sherry would give her something she didn't really like.

"Boodle, eat it up," they would command her. "It's good for you."

Boodle would sniff it and turn her head away. "Eat it up," they would say again. And finally she would pick it up and swallow it in one big gulp. Dena and Sherry would tell her what a good dog she was, and she would be as happy as if they had given her a favorite doggie treat.

Later, when the family moved to the Philippines, for breakfast everyone usually had a big slice of delicious papaya along with lots of other fruit. Sometimes a slice of that good papaya would be missing from a plate. Where could it have gone? No one knew for sure.

Then one morning Mommy went into the dining room early, and at that very moment, a piece of papaya disappeared over the edge of the table. She knew at once who had done it.

"Boodle, come here," she called; and poor Boodle knew Mommy wasn't happy. She quickly swallowed the papaya—skin and all—and then slowly went around the table for the scolding she knew she deserved.

After that, their helper put the papaya where Boodle couldn't reach it.

But while the family was still in Singapore, Boodle's

mouth got her into big trouble one day. The family had bought a little snow-white parakeet, and also a nice big cage for it. They wanted it to be able to fly around some-times, so Mommy learned how to clip the feathers on its wings so it couldn't fly so high that they couldn't catch it.

It took quite a while to decide on a name for their new little pet. One time, Sherry said, "It's so darling."

"That's what we'll call her," Dena said right away. "We'll call her Darling." So Darling was her name from then on.

Boodle was very interested in Darling. One day when the girls let Darling out of her cage, she flew right over Boodle's head. Instantly, Boodle jumped up and caught the bird in her mouth. Everyone saw it happen, and everyone screamed at once. They were sure their precious pet had been killed.

Boodle froze with Darling still in her mouth, and Mommy went to see if she could get her out. "Give her to me," she told Boodle while the girls held their breath. Boodle opened her mouth at once and let Mommy take Darling out. She hadn't been hurt at all.

Everyone had forgotten that Boodle was a spaniel, and spaniels are bird dogs that can easily catch birds without killing them. Boodle couldn't understand why there was so much excitement, but she knew she must never touch Darling again. And she never did.

Boodle Stays Behind

"We have been here in Singapore for five years, so now it's time for us to take a furlough," Daddy announced one day.

"What will we do while we're gone?" Dena and Sherry wanted to know. Daddy explained that they would go back to the United States for a year. They would see many new places on the way; they would visit their grandpas and grandmas and many other relatives; and they would probably all go to school.

"Can we take Boodle?" was the next question.

"No, we can't take Boodle," Mommy told them. "But the Wilcoxes want to keep her for us until we come back."

Elder Wilcox was a Bible teacher at the school, and Dena and Sherry agreed that if they couldn't take Boodle with them, Grandpa and Grandma Wilcox were the best people they could think of to keep their precious pet.

Boodle didn't pay much attention to the packing and getting ready to leave that went on day after day. She wasn't worrying about anything, but the girls were. They were very sure that Boodle would miss them a lot.

One day Mommy invited the Wilcoxes over to eat lunch. Grandma Wilcox sat at the end of the table, and Boodle was close by, as usual. Pretty soon, the family noticed that Boodle was sitting right beside Grandma Wilcox all the time. Her tail was thumping on the floor, and she had her doggie smile on her face as she kept looking up at the kind lady beside her.

Suddenly, Mommy was sure she knew just what was happening. "Are you feeding Boodle some of your food?"

she asked with a smile. Grandma Wilcox smiled back and winked.

"No wonder Boodle is already falling in love with you," Mommy laughed. "We never feed her anything at the table, so she is having a wonderful treat today."

Grandma Wilcox explained that she wanted Boodle to get used to her so she wouldn't be too lonely after the girls and the rest of the family left.

Dena and Sherry looked at each other, and then at Boodle. They didn't know whether they should be happy or sad. They were too polite to say anything about what they were thinking, but after their company left they talked about it.

Would Boodle forget them while they were away? They didn't want her to be too lonely, but they didn't want her to forget them, either. Finally they decided to be glad for Boodle's sake, even though they were sure they would miss her a lot.

Anyway, they would have lots of fun on their long trip across the ocean between Singapore and North America. And they would also be busy going to school. Some other kind people wanted to keep Darling, their funny little para-keet, so everything was going to be just fine.

When the time came to sail away, they waved good-by to their friends, and knew they had many, many things for which to thank God.

While Dena and Sherry and their parents were visiting people and going to school in the United States, Boodle was living with the Wilcoxes in Singapore. Grandma Wilcox wrote interesting letters about her.

"Boodle is happy," she told them. "And she makes us happy, too. When someone knocks at the door, she tries to jump up and run at the same time, but she slips and slides on the slippery floor before she gets going, and it looks so funny."

The girls laughed when they read that. Boodle did the same in their house in Singapore. In fact, at mealtime Daddy would often call "Come in!" like he always did when someone knocked at the door.

The whole family knew that no one was at the door; but Boodle didn't know that. She would jump up and try to get to the door as fast as she could. She would slip and slide and even tumble over on the slippery floor while everyone laughed at her. Then she would come back with a happy doggie smile on her face.

One day someone came to talk to Daddy. The man said that Daddy was needed to help in a big school in the Philippines. That was a long way from Singapore; and when Daddy said he was willing to go, of course all the family's plans changed.

Dena and Sherry were worried. "How will we get Boodle back?" they wanted to know. But Mommy and Daddy didn't have an answer. Nobody knew.

After the family arrived in the Philippines, another letter

came from Grandpa and Grandma Wilcox. "We are going to leave Singapore sooner than we expected," the letter said; "and of course we are wondering what we should do about Boodle and Darling.

"We have found out that Ethel Young is going to the Philippines by ship, and she is willing to take Boodle and Darling with her, if you would like that. You can meet them at the ship and take Boodle and Darling to your home.

"Grandpa Wilcox will make a big, strong crate [a wooden box] to keep Boodle in while they travel, and Miss Young will make sure she has food and water and some exercise every day. Please let us know what you think of this idea."

"Oh goody! We have a way to get Boodle and Darling back!" Dena and Sherry were very happy, and their parents were, too.

They counted the days until the ship would come from Singapore with their pets. Those days couldn't go by fast enough, but finally the ship arrived and the girls and their parents went to meet it.

"Will Boodle remember us?" they wondered.

Boodle Joins Her Family

Dena and Sherry and their parents were watching as passengers on the big ship from Singapore walked down the gangplank. "There she is," they called as they saw Miss Young, and they all waved to her.

But Miss Young was holding Boodle's leash with one hand and Darling's cage with the other, so she couldn't wave back.

"Boodle! Boodle!" the girls called, and Boodle picked up her ears and looked toward them, whining and pulling on her leash. As soon as she was close enough, Miss Young let Boodle off the leash and everyone laughed as Boodle ran to the family. She hadn't forgotten them.

Back in the car, they all talked at once. "She's so fat." "She remembered us." "What's wrong with Boodle's fur? It isn't soft any more. It feels rough." "Grandma Wilcox was too good to you, Boodle." "We're going to have to put you on a diet."

Boodle didn't care what they were saying about her. She was happy to be back with the family again.

Miss Young said the sailors on the ship all loved Boodle. One of the officers decided she shouldn't have to stay in the wooden box, so he let her out, and took care of her in his nice cabin. The sailors took her for walks on the decks, and made sure she had lots of food. Miss Young didn't have to worry one minute about Boodle; and she enjoyed little Darling, too.

At home, Boodle had a different house and yard to check out. She snooped and sniffed everywhere, while the girls watched her and planned with Mommy how to help her lose weight and get her soft, silky fur back again.

When they took her for a walk to meet the other missionaries and some of the many students, she wagged her tail and was friendly and polite to everyone.

"Wait until you see her after she isn't so fat, and her fur gets nice again," the girls told them.

It took a while, but she finally did get to look like her old self again, and everyone agreed that she was a very beautiful dog.

Darling soon got used to her new home, too. Her cage was right by a big window in the kitchen, and she had lots of room to fly around when the cage door was opened. She still wasn't afraid of Boodle; but whenever she landed on Boodle, the dog would stand perfectly still and keep her head down until Darling flew away. She never forgot the day she caught Darling in her mouth and the scolding she got.

The Philippines was hot like Singapore; but there was a wonderful, cool place not too far away. The family didn't have a big car anymore; but their little Volkswagen could hold them all, including Boodle; so vacations were fun for everyone.

Boodle's Vacation

"We're going to Baguio. We're going to Baguio." Dena and Sherry sang as they held hands and jumped up and down while Boodle yapped happily and ran around and around them in circles as if she knew just what they were saying.

The weather in Manila was very hot, but in Baguio it was so cool they always had to take sweaters and warm clothes. No wonder the family enjoyed being there for a few days, even though the trip took about four hours and their car wasn't air conditioned! Best of all, Boodle always got to go, too.

"Are you sure we need sweaters this time, Mommy?" Dena asked. "It's so hot here in Manila."

"You always say that when we're packing for Baguio," Mommy reminded Dena. "But you're always glad for sweaters when we get there." So the sweaters went with them as usual.

But that wasn't all. The girls made sure they packed their little folding lamp, a rug to lay in front of the fireplace in their cabin, some cushions, a little clock, flower vases, pretty doilies, and some of their favorite games and books, too. Mommy packed sheets, warm blankets, food, and clothes.

One time when they had to go by train to Baguio, Mommy had said she was sure there wouldn't be room for the extra things they always took to make their cabin cozy. But Dena and Sherry quietly packed the "extras" in a big basket that they carried between them, and Mommy didn't even notice until they were on the train.

Those "extras" were very important to Dena and Sherry. And other people enjoyed them, too. "Your cabin is always so cozy," they would say. "How do you manage to bring all those things in your little Volkswagen?"

"Besides the car trunk [under the hood], we make the floor in the back seat into a trunk, too," the girls would explain. "We put the pillows and an old blanket on top, and then we sit on top of it all."

This trip to Baguio was going to be extra special, because Daddy had promised to drive along the seashore on the way. They would get to swim and play in the sand, so swimming clothes and buckets and shovels went into the little car, too. And finally they were on their way.

Boodle sat in the back with Dena and Sherry, trying to see everything at the same time. She stuck her head over Daddy's shoulder to see ahead, but Daddy didn't like her doggie kisses and drooling on his shirt. Then she put her head out the side windows in the back. Her ears flapped in the wind and she yapped a happy hello to the many dogs in the villages they drove through.

Then, finally, they arrived at the beautiful beach.

Boodle Goes Swimming

Dena, Sherry, Mommy, Daddy, and Boodle had finally arrived at the beach on their way to cool Baguio. Boodle didn't need a bathing suit, so she rushed ahead to the water while the rest changed one by one as best they could inside their little car. Because she was part water spaniel, Boodle liked swimming.

While the family was changing, Boodle rushed back and forth from the water to the car as if to say, "Why are the rest of you taking so long?" But finally they were all with her in the water.

Soon the family went out far enough to hold hands and jump the waves as they rolled in. That was so much fun; but for some reason, Boodle panicked. She never took her eyes off of the ocean as she rushed back and forth on the beach, barking as loudly as she could. Finally, she swam out to them and made sure she bumped each one of them with her nose. Then she swam back to shore and started barking again.

"What's wrong with Boodle? Why is she acting like that?" the girls wanted to know.

Daddy laughed. "I think she's too close to the ground to be able to see us over the waves, and that probably makes her worried. She swims out and touches each of us to make sure that we're all safe." And Daddy was probably right.

Boodle was a lot happier when the family got tired of swimming and jumping waves, and decided to play in the sand for a while. While the girls built sand castles and hunted for shells, Boodle dug her own holes or raced up and down the beach.

Finally, it was time to start up the mountain to cool Baguio and the mountain cabin. The family washed as much sand off as they could and put their traveling clothes back on. They made Boodle shake and shake, and dried her fur and paws. And they were all so tired, only Daddy kept awake because he was driving. Even Boodle fell asleep.

When they got to the cabin, it felt good to take showers and wash off the sand and salt water. Even Boodle didn't mind being clean again. "I'm glad we brought sweaters," Dena told Mommy. Soon a fire was going in the fire-place; everything was unpacked and put away. The cabin was cozy and warm, and Mommy read a Bible story for worship. They thanked God for the safe trip and the fun they had at the beach.

Everyone was glad to crawl into bed and pull the warm blankets around their ears. Boodle was already asleep on the rug in front of the fireplace.

There would be many more trips and interesting, fun-filled days ahead that Boodle and the family would enjoy together. But, of course, Boodle didn't know that. She was just being a happy pet that the family and many others loved.

Two Special Birds

Dena and Sherry's parents were teaching them to be respectful, and so they didn't call other missionaries by their first names. Instead, they always called them "Uncle" or "Auntie."

Uncle Jack and Auntie Olivine were special friends of Dena, Sherry, and their parents. One day when they were visiting, Uncle Jack asked, "Don't you think your pet bird Darling needs a mate so she won't be lonely?"

Darling, a white parakeet, had never seemed even a little bit lonely; but Dena and Sherry were excited about the idea of having another pet. Sherry had tried more than once to sneak a big toad into one of their wash tubs, but Mommy had always found them and they would have to go back outside.

"Darling is in a nice large cage," Mommy agreed, "so we have plenty of room for a second bird. What's her name?"

"It isn't a her," Auntie Olivine said. "It's a he, and we've been calling him Pretty Boy. He is very tame, and he has even learned to talk a little bit."

The girls were delighted. They had tried and tried to coax Darling to talk, but she wouldn't cooperate. She could twitter happily and scold when she felt like it; but no matter how hard they tried, she wouldn't talk "people talk"— just "bird talk." Perhaps Pretty Boy could coax her to learn.

"What can Pretty Boy say?" the girls wanted to know.

"Well, he says, 'I can talk people talk, can you talk, talk, talk?'" Uncle Jack laughed. "He's supposed to say, 'Can you talk bird talk?' but so far he doesn't want to learn the rest of what he's supposed to say."

Everyone thought that was very funny.

The family wanted to know all about Pretty Boy. "What color is he?" they asked next. They were pleased when Auntie Olivine said his feathers were a beautiful green.

"Because we'll be going back to the United States soon, we need to find a home for Pretty Boy, and we thought of you; and it sounds like you want to have him." And the whole family said "Yes" at the same time.

When they brought Pretty Boy and put him into the big cage, the two birds looked at each other for a little while. Then Pretty Boy hopped up onto the other end of the long perch Darling was on. Very slowly he moved closer and closer to her, twittering a friendly birdie "Hello." Darling didn't move.

Finally, Pretty Boy was sitting right beside her. Darling tipped her head to one side and watched him carefully. Then smart little Pretty Bird said right in Darling's ear, "I'm a pretty bird. I can..."

But before he could finish, Darling gave him a peck that really didn't hurt him at all, but scared him so badly that he flew to another perch and sat there thinking about what had happened.

The family couldn't help laughing. They weren't worried. They knew Darling and Pretty Boy would learn to get along very well. And they did.

Pretty Boy and Darling

Pretty Boy's wing feathers were clipped like Darling's, and he enjoyed getting out of the cage often for some exercise. When one of the family held out a finger near him, he would step gently onto it, twittering and talking. The family really loved him. But Darling was something else.

The door of the bird cage had to be lifted up to clean and refill the water and food dishes inside, or to let the birds out to fly around for a while. But when the catch on the door stopped working, the door wouldn't stay open by itself; and someone would have to hold it open.

Darling didn't like waiting for anything. She soon figured out that if she put her beak around the bottom of the cage door and tossed her head up, she could open the door. If she did that trick quickly enough, she could fly out before the door dropped down again. If she didn't, the door would drop down on top of her before she got all the way out.

That didn't hurt her, but as she wiggled and pushed her way out, she would scold as if what happened was someone else's fault.

Pretty Boy would watch it all, but he never once tried to open that door. He was a very polite little bird compared to Darling.

One thing Darling loved to do got her in trouble more than once. She liked riding around on Mommy's shoulder while she was busy in the kitchen. One time when the sink was full of fluffy soap suds, they looked so harmless and interesting that Darling decided to dive right into them.

38

Mommy scooped her out at once, but Darling sneezed, shook her head, and scolded as if what happened was Mommy's fault.

Another time, Darling was leaning way out as she sat on Mommy's shoulder. She didn't want to miss what was happening. "You could get into big trouble if you're too curious," Mommy warned Darling as she put a handful of chopped onions into a hot frying pan. Sure enough, Darling suddenly lost her balance and tumbled right into the frying pan.

Mommy instantly got her out and carefully checked to see if her little feet were burned. Thankfully, they were all right; but, as usual, Darling scolded as if her fall was Mommy's fault.

Dena or Sherry often turned the kitchen faucet on so the water ran out in a tiny stream. Darling was sure that the tiny stream must be some sort of string hanging from the faucet, and she never gave up trying to grab it.

One thing the girls discovered was how to give their little pets a bath. They put some water into big bowls, and then added bits of torn-up lettuce. Pretty Boy and Darling would hop into the lettuce and flutter around, splashing the water and getting themselves all wet. Back in their cage, they fluffed and preened their feathers, carefully smoothing them all back in place.

Darling Tries to Read

"Darling, you're naughty!" Sherry stamped her foot and waved a big feather duster at Darling who was running back and forth along a little ledge near the dining room ceiling.

The girls wanted to go outside to play, but no one was supposed to open the front door when the birds were out of their cage. It would be too easy for them to fly away and get lost.

Darling cocked her head and looked down at Sherry as if to say, "I'm not scared of that feather duster. I'll come down when I'm ready!" And finally she did.

It was obviously time to clip Darling's wing feathers again, and doing that didn't hurt at all. But Darling always seemed to know she wouldn't be able to fly as high afterwards, so she would scold and try to peck Mommy whenever clipping time came.

One day as Dena and Sherry were playing with a large cardboard tube (like the tubes gift-wrapping paper comes on), they had a bright idea. "Let's put it on the floor, and coax the birds to go through it!" So they brought both little pets to where they were playing.

When Dena put Pretty Boy at one end, he looked down the tube. Then he turned and walked away. Darling was next. She peered inside the tube. At the other end, Sherry called, "Come on, Darling!" and Darling quickly ran to her.

"What a smart little bird! Tell her to go back!" Dena said. Sherry turned Darling around and the bird hurried back through the tube to Dena. Both girls laughed and praised her. Darling had learned another trick, and the family enjoyed it many times after that.

Mommy graded her students' papers and wrote letters while she sat at her big desk. Darling usually enjoyed sitting on her shoulder and looking around. But one day she noticed something for the first time. She leaned way over and watched for awhile. Then she hopped down onto the desk for a closer look.

Finally Darling walked even closer and watched carefully as Mommy wrote with her red pen. Mommy wished she knew what the little bird was thinking. Did Darling wonder what was coming out of that pen? Maybe she thought it looked like a little red thread.

When Darling started trying to pick up the red letters, Mommy burst out laughing and called Dena and Sherry.

"Watch Darling," she told the girls as she put a new piece of paper down and wrote on it. At once Darling started doing her best to pick up what she was sure was some strange, pretty thread; and they all had a good laugh.

Darling never did figure out that the "thread" that came out of Mommy's pen was really ink.

It seemed as if Darling would never run out of surprises for the family, but one morning she gave them the biggest one of all.

Darling's Surprise

What's wrong with Darling?" the girls wanted to know one evening. Darling was not acting like her usual self. Mommy came to the cage and looked at Darling, too.

"I don't know," Mommy said thoughtfully. "I noticed she wasn't acting like herself this afternoon. I don't think she's sick, but she's been huddling down there in one corner of the cage for a long time; and she hasn't even once tried to toss the cage door up so she could fly out."

"I know," Sherry said. "When I reached in and tried to pick her up a little while ago, she wouldn't let me. She just pecked at me."

"Well, she hasn't stopped eating her food and drinking her water, so I don't think we need to worry about her—at least not yet," Mommy decided. "But if she's really getting sick, Pretty Boy will probably get sick, too."

At worship, they prayed for Darling, and then the girls went to bed as usual. But in the morning, they both hurried to the bird cage to check on their little pets. They were happy to see both birds sitting on their perches looking and acting as usual. Darling wasn't huddling in the corner of the cage and seemed perfectly normal.

Later, Mommy came into the kitchen. She was glad that both birds were as perky as ever. But then she saw something the girls hadn't noticed.

"Dena! Sherry!" Mommy called. "Come see what's in the cage. I can't believe it!"

Both girls ran into the kitchen. "What are we supposed to see?"

"Look carefully. It's down in the corner where Darling was huddled last night," Mommy told them.

When Dena and Sherry looked, they couldn't believe their eyes. "It's an egg!" they shouted. "Darling laid an egg!" They jumped for joy and praised Darling as if she had done the most wonderful thing in the world.

But Mommy soon calmed them down. "Carefully pick up the little egg and see if it's warm," she told them.

Gently, they picked up the tiny egg. It was cold. How disappointed they were when Mommy said that Darling's egg couldn't possibly hatch. For a long time they kept the little egg anyway, but finally they got over how sorry they had felt.

At bedtime or nap time, both birds tucked their heads under their fluffy wings, closed their eyes, and quickly fell asleep without any fussing. They never complained about their cage or their food or the weather or about being bored. Wherever they were, they were content. How about you? Are you learning to choose to be happy?

Darling and Pretty Boy gave the family many happy memories, and taught Dena and Sherry many important lessons. They learned how God cares for children even more than He cares about birds.

They also learned that Darling wasn't to blame because she got into trouble so many times, but children must learn to obey if they are going to be happy and make God and others happy, too.

A Sad Letter

Dena and Sherry had grown a lot taller by the time the family went on their second furlough. In fact, Sherry had grown taller than Dena; and often people who didn't know them thought she was the older. Dena didn't always like that, but they were still best friends.

"What is going to happen to our dog Boodle and our birds?" they wanted to know.

"Well, you already know there are many people who would like to take care of them for us," Daddy reminded the girls.

"Yes, but we aren't sure who would be the best ones," they said. And it really was hard to decide. Finally, they chose a lovely Chinese family who wanted to keep Boodle in their nice house. Dena and Sherry knew they would take good care of her.

When the day came for Boodle to leave, the Chinese family drove up in their car. Since Boodle loved riding in a car, she wagged her tail and jumped right into the car when the Chinese lady asked her if she wanted a ride. Off they went, waving good-by. But Daddy, Mommy, Dena, and Sherry had a hard time keeping the tears back. They couldn't help feeling sad.

Soon the family left on furlough, and they were very glad that the Chinese family wrote letters to them while they were traveling in other countries on their way back to the United States.

One day, they stopped at a place where they knew mail would be waiting for them. It was getting close to lunch time, but they decided they wanted to read their letters first. When they saw a letter from the Chinese family taking care of Boodle, they couldn't wait to read it.

Mommy opened the letter and started reading. Then she stopped. Her eyes had run ahead and she couldn't go on.

"Keep reading!" Daddy and the girls told her. They were impatient to hear about Boodle. But Mommy couldn't.

"What's wrong?" the girls wanted to know. Then, "Has something happened to Boodle?"

Mommy nodded, and finally she was able to read the rest of the letter. Boodle had suddenly gotten very sick, and nothing the kind family could do helped. Very quickly she had died. The Chinese family felt terrible and were so very sorry.

Now everyone in the car was crying. Even Daddy could hardly drive. No one was hungry anymore, so they just skipped eating lunch. Their dear, precious dog Boodle was gone. It was very hard to believe they would never see her again.

At first the girls wondered why God had let Boodle die. Every day they had asked Him to take care of her. But their parents reminded them that God always knows what is best, and that He cared about Boodle, too.

"When we get to heaven," the girls decided, "Maybe God will have another dog waiting, just exactly like Boodle, and it will rush to meet us." Daddy smiled, and Mommy thought that just might happen.

No More Pets!

"I've decided there will be no more pets!" Daddy announced one day after Boodle died. "We get too attached to them. Anyway, you girls will be going away to school, and won't be home like you have been in the past."

No one argued with Daddy.

While the family was on furlough in the United States, the mission asked Daddy to go back to the Philippines and be the business manager of the hospital in Manila. That meant the family would be moving to another place, and they would have new neighbors.

Dena was old enough to go to the school for missionary children in Singapore; and at the end of her first year there, Sherry decided to go with Dena. The day before they left, two other girls who were planning to go to that school came and stayed at their house. They would all fly together on an airplane the next day.

Very early the next morning, Mommy went to the market to buy food. As she stepped outside she heard a very tiny "Mew."

"Oh, no!" Mommy thought. "I'm not even going to look to find out where that sound came from."

When she came back, their neighbor looked out of his back door. "Good morning!" he greeted her. "I'm not sure, but I think I heard a little sound that makes me think someone has dropped a kitten over the wall into your back yard."

Mommy felt like saying, "Oh, no!" but she just smiled,

even though she didn't feel like it. "Well, the street on the other side is right beside the wall, and it's easy to toss something over," she said pleasantly as she carried the baskets of food upstairs.

The girls were still sleeping; but since Daddy had to be at work soon, Daddy and Mommy started eating breakfast without them. Suddenly, Daddy stopped and looked out the big window behind the table.

"I think I can hear a kitten mewing," he said. "I think... well, I can't actually see it, but come look." Mommy pushed back her chair and looked, too.

"Look under that big leaf right down there," Daddy pointed. "Don't you see something tiny and pink opening and closing?"

Mommy sighed. "Dena! Sherry!" she called, "Daddy thinks someone has dropped a kitten over the wall into our back yard."

The girls didn't have to be called twice. They were downstairs at the back door in seconds. "Kitty, kitty! Come, kitty!" they called even though they couldn't really see it. And out from under the big leaf, a tiny black kitten came hopping across the lawn right to them and snuggled in their warm hands.

"I cannot let this happen," Mommy told herself. "The girls are leaving this very day, and I don't have time to train and care for such a tiny kitten! Someone else will have to take care of it. I know Daddy will agree. After all, he was the one who said, 'No more pets!' "

47

A Tiny Black Kitten

Look, Mommy, isn't it darling?" The tiny black kitten that had been dropped over their back wall purred happily as it cuddled in their warm hands. "We'll make a litter box and a place for it to sleep, and everything!" Dena and Sherry promised. "It won't be any trouble at all."

Mommy eyed the kitten. It really was cute; but she decided to stay firm about not keeping it. "Fixing a litter box doesn't guarantee it's going to always use it," she reminded them. "You both know it takes time to train a pet, and you know how busy I am."

But at least the girls got to keep the kitten until they left that afternoon; then, Mommy was sure, she could find a home for it. Very soon there was a litter box and a bed for the kitten on the landing of the inside stairs that went down to the basement.

"Now this is where you go every time!" the kitten was told, "You can't ever make a mess anywhere in the house. You have to be a very obedient kitten!" And, believe it or not, it seemed to understand every word they said.

"Help us decide what to name it," the girls told their two friends. As the kitten eagerly lapped warm milk from a little saucer, they suggested different names. Finally, everyone decided to call it Spooky because it was black, it couldn't be seen in the dark, and it had suddenly arrived from nobody knew where.

Mommy had planned to stay home that day, and she could hardly believe that every time the kitten needed to use the litter box, it hopped all the way from the girls' bedroom at one corner of the big house to the litter box at the opposite corner. Then it hopped all the way back to play with the girls.

When Daddy came home for lunch, the girls were all talking about Spooky. Daddy just smiled, and Mommy reminded them of the "No more pets" decision that had been made after Boodle died.

At the airport, along with Dena's and Sherry's hugs and tears, they asked about Spooky. "Please keep him," they begged. "We'll be gone nine whole months, and he'll be a beautiful big cat when we get back, but you can tell us about him in your letters every week; so, please?"

Mommy and Daddy still didn't promise. "We'll see," was all they would say before they waved good-by to their girls. They sadly watched until the airplane lifted off the ground and flew away.

Back home, the house seemed very, very empty—except for Spooky. He had had a fun-filled day, and when Mommy put him into the soft bed the girls had made for him, he snuggled down and fell sound asleep.

Spooky Joins the Family

"Well, what are we going to do about Spooky?" Mommy asked Daddy as they ate breakfast all alone the morning after the girls left for the school in Singapore.

The living room and dining room were all one large room, and they both had to smile as they watched Spooky chase a little, wadded-up paper ball around the big room. Eppie, their Filipino helper, had already met the kitten and liked him. She came from the kitchen and called, "Spooky, come! You have bread and milk for breakfast!"

Spooky ran to the kitchen and ate his breakfast. By the time Daddy left for work, he still hadn't answered Mommy's question. Eppie hurried off to her classes. And Mommy had so much to do in the office building close by. What should she do with the tiny kitten while she was gone?

Mommy decided to shut all the bedroom and bathroom doors. Then, she looked at Spooky.

"I don't know if I can trust you here alone," she told him as she picked him up. He snuggled against her and purred. "You are lovable," she added. "But that doesn't mean we can keep you; and I know other families that would take you in a minute." She sighed as she gently put Spooky down, went out the door, and closed it behind her.

At noon, Mommy hurried home and looked around. Spooky had been sound asleep on a living room chair. He stood up, stretched, arched his tiny back, hopped down, and ran to her. She picked him up and went to the kitchen where Eppie was fixing lunch.

"Has Spooky behaved while we were gone?" Mommy asked.

"Oh yes, Ma'am," Eppie answered politely. "Spooky is using his litter box like he is supposed to. I think everything is fine."

Soon Daddy came in. "Well, I see Spooky is still here," he said as the tiny kitten rubbed against his pant legs and discovered that his shoelaces moved when he gave them a little swat with his paws.

"Yes, Spooky is still here and you need to decide what to do next," Mommy reminded him.

Daddy sat down to eat, and thought some more. When he finally answered, she was sure that Spooky would be a new member of the family. "The girls really want us to keep him, don't they?" he said.

"Yes, they do," Mommy agreed.

"Well, I suppose it will be alright to keep him, if you don't mind."

Mommy laughed. "I don't mind, and the girls will be very pleased," she said. So Spooky became part of the family.

And just as the girls said, the tiny kitten grew fast; and in a few months he became a beautiful cat. People who got acquainted with Spooky didn't soon forget him. He had many friends.

Dena and Sherry could hardly wait to get home to see him, especially when they read about all the special tricks he was learning. Keep reading to find out more about what Spooky was learning to do.

Nobody Owns a Cat

Have you ever heard someone say that a dog is man's best friend? Most dogs are very faithful, and they forgive us even when we hurt them. But cats are very different from dogs.

There is a saying that nobody owns a cat. That means that cats usually do what they please, not what their owners want them to do.

Well, Spooky was a cat. In his special way he loved his family, but that didn't mean he always obeyed. Daddy and Mommy were glad that he quickly learned to never scratch his claws on the furniture. And he was very good about staying at home. But if they didn't watch when the front door opened, he would sneak out every time.

From the front door of the house, steps went down to a landing; then the steps went on down to the ground. Whenever Spooky got outside, he would always stop at the landing.

"Spooky, come back!" Mommy would say firmly. Spooky would look up, roll onto his back, and wiggle contentedly as if to say, "I'll come when I get ready, thank you." If they didn't want to keep standing there in the doorway waiting for him to come in, they had to go down to the landing, pick him up, and carry him back into the house—which was probably just what he wanted.

Whenever he got a little swat for being naughty, he'd jump onto the back of a chair where he could look out a big window and keep track of everything that was happening outside.

One time Spooky disappeared, and even though Mommy called, she couldn't find him anywhere. Finally someone pointed and said, "Look at Spooky!" There he was, on the top of the door! That happened more than once, but they could never figure out how he got up that high, or how he kept from falling off of something so narrow.

Another trick he learned was a lot of fun. Mommy would look down at Spooky and hold out her hands to him. "Jump, Spooky!" she would tell him. Spooky would stand up, wiggle a bit, and then jump right into her arms. Of course Mommy praised and cuddled him while his loud purring showed how much he enjoyed the attention she was giving him.

One day, some friends gave the family another animal, but it wasn't alive. It was a large, beautiful carabao carved out of wood. A carabao looks a lot like a cow with long horns.

Spooky looked at the carabao, then walked over and sniffed it all over. Then he finally walked away and didn't bother with it anymore. But one day someone accidentally knocked against it and the end of one of its horns fell onto the floor.

Spooky pushed the broken piece of horn with his paws, but it wasn't fun to play with, so he walked away. He didn't like that animal very much, anyway. And later, they found out how much he didn't like it.

Spooky and the Carabao

Someone had given Dena and Sherry's family a large carved carabao, but one of its wooden horns had broken off. So Daddy got some strong glue and stuck the horn back on, and no one could tell it had broken. But Spooky knew it had.

One day he walked over, looked at the carabao, lifted his paw, and swatted that horn hard. What do you think happened? The horn fell off again.

It didn't matter how hard Daddy tried to glue that horn on, or how much Spooky was scolded. Nothing kept him from hitting it again. Finally the family just let the horn lie beside the poor carabao, and loved Spooky anyway.

One evening, Daddy was sitting in a comfortable chair in the living room. He had one foot resting on the knee of his other leg, and that made a big hole. When he looked down, there sat Spooky looking up at him through the hole.

"Come on, Spooky! Jump!" he invited, beckoning with his hand. Spooky didn't need a second invitation. He jumped through the hole and landed right on Daddy's lap. He had learned a new trick.

After that, if Daddy was sitting that way, holding a magazine or newspaper in front of him, Spooky would jump up and crash into the newspaper or magazine. Daddy was always surprised, but he'd laugh. He thought Spooky had learned a very clever trick.

When men came to visit and sat the way Daddy often did, they almost always got a big surprise. Spooky would suddenly jump between their legs and sit on their lap. It made them laugh, and they never forgot that funny black cat.

Spooky was pleased when he discovered he could play the piano. He had heard Mommy playing it many times, but he had never tried it himself. But one day when the piano lid was open, Spooky jumped up onto the piano bench, lifted his paw, and laid it on a key. It made a sound!

Hmmm. That was very nice, so Spooky did it again and again. Then he must have wondered what would happen if he put all his paws on the keys. So he stepped onto the piano keyboard; and sure enough, there were many sounds. When he walked carefully from one end to the other, the sounds went from very high like birds singing, to very low like a dog growling.

Spooky enjoyed playing the piano. He couldn't open the lid, but when it was left open, he liked to play his own concert.

The family never forgot one time when a special speaker from the United States was staying with them. The speaker could play the piano very well, and he and Spooky became good friends. But he didn't know that Spooky could play, too, until one day...

Spooky Plays the Piano

One day the guest heard soft sounds coming from the piano; but from where he was sitting, he could see that no one was sitting at the piano bench. He stood up and looked, but he still couldn't see anyone. Finally, he walked around to where he could see the keyboard; and there was Spooky walking carefully from one end to the other.

The guest laughed and laughed because he thought it was so funny.

On Sabbath, the guest had to speak at a big meeting being held at the college, and Mommy drove him there right after breakfast. She went back in time to drive him home after the evening meeting.

"You have had a long day," Mommy said. "You must be very tired."

The guest admitted that he was very tired. Then Mommy said, "Well, at least you met many interesting people today, I'm sure."

"Yes, I've met many interesting people," the guest told her. Then he chuckled as he added, "But I didn't meet anyone as interesting as Spooky, your black cat."

The guest and Mommy both laughed. There was no doubt about it; Spooky was a very interesting cat.

It seemed as if Spooky was especially active on Sabbaths. The family almost always invited others to eat Sabbath dinner with them, and Spooky made sure the visitors knew that he was part of the family, too.

One Sabbath while the visitors were sitting in the living

room with the family, Spooky walked into the middle of the room and stood there. Then, he looked up at the ceiling and noticed the fan. Everyone watched as he stared at the blades going around and around.

Soon Spooky started walking around and around on the floor under the fan, tipping his head so he could see it. As he circled around on the floor, he lifted his paw, making a swatting motion as if he were trying to make the fan stop. By then everyone was laughing at the silly cat; and of course Spooky was enjoying entertaining them.

One Sabbath when Dena and Sherry were at home on vacation, Spooky interrupted the conversation after dinner so badly that Sherry finally picked him up and announced, "Spooky, you're being naughty and I'm going to put you where you can't bother us!" Then she put Spooky in the bathroom and shut the door.

"There! Now we can have a little peace!" Sherry said. And for a few minutes there was peace—but not for long. Suddenly, crashing sounds started coming from the bathroom, and Mommy and Sherry hurried to see what was happening. Most cats would have started meowing loudly, but not Spooky. He had thought of a much faster way to get what he wanted.

Naughty Spooky

When Mommy and Sherry opened the door, there sat Spooky in the open space between the drawers and the shelves above it, looking innocent. On the floor were the things that had been sitting neatly in the open space. Spooky had purposely knocked all of them off the shelf. Some things were broken; some had spilled. It was a mess.

Of course Spooky was scolded, but he ran out to the living room, looked around, and then went on through the dining room and kitchen to his food dish. After eating a snack, he stretched out for a nap.

Everyone thought it was all really funny, but the next Sabbath the family made sure that the things in that open space were safely behind closed doors in the cupboard right above it.

"Now," they thought, "Spooky can't reach anything."

It wasn't many weeks before Spooky was put in the bathroom again. This time, the family relaxed as everyone visited in peace—for awhile. When they heard those same crashing noises again, the family couldn't believe it; and Mommy hurried to see what had happened this time. Again, Spooky was sitting in the open space, looking innocent.

Cats have a wonderful ability to smell, and probably Spooky had jumped up and found the open space empty. Perhaps his nose told him that what he wanted was behind the closed doors above him. Somehow, Spooky reached with his paw and got the cupboard door open. Then, probably he jumped into the cupboard from the floor, and right there in front of him was everything he was trying to find.

That was the last time Spooky got put into the bathroom. From then on, when he was a bother he had to go to the basement where he could prowl around as much as he pleased.

By now, the girls were back in the United States learning to be nurses. They were always impatient for news from home. Learning what Spooky had been doing was such fun.

Then Mommy learned that her daddy (Dena and Sherry's grandpa) was dying. She traveled back to her parents' home in Canada. The family was very sad. Daddy and Spooky were alone in the Philippines until furlough time came again.

Daddy wondered what he would do with Spooky during furlough. All their friends knew and loved the funny black cat, and it was hard to choose where to leave him. Finally, Daddy decided where to leave Spooky, and then he flew in an airplane to be with Mommy and the girls.

As usual, time went by very fast. When it was time to fly back to the Philippines again, Grandma was with them. She missed her husband very much, but she had happy memories of being missionaries with him in India and Burma many years before. And now she was very glad to be a missionary again.

It didn't take long to get settled, and then it was time to have Spooky come back.

Good-by Spooky

Mommy and Daddy, along with Grandma, were settled in the Philippines again and were already at work. Daddy had made sure the horn belonging to the carved carabao was on so well that it wouldn't come off anymore. And now it was time for Spooky to be back with them.

One day the front door opened. A hand reached in and dropped Spooky onto the floor. "Here's Spooky!" the missionaries laughed as they followed him. He had a bright red ribbon around his neck and he stood still as he looked around.

Right away he saw the carved carabao.

At once, Spooky walked over to the carabao, raised his paw, and hit the horn that he had always been able to knock off. When it didn't fall, he seemed puzzled. Then he turned and jumped up to the very same spot where he always sat and watched what was happening outside. He acted just as if he had never been away.

Grandma had heard all about Spooky, and they became best friends. When Sherry finished learning to be a nurse, she came home to the Philippines to rest a while and be with the family. They all missed Dena, but they wrote many letters to her.

One day, Spooky didn't seem as frisky as usual. Little by little he seemed to be more and more lazy. The family wondered what was the matter. Sherry, Mommy, and Daddy were all nurses, and Grandma had taken care of lots of sick people; but none of them could figure out what was wrong with their precious pet.

Finally, they decided to take Spooky to a good animal doctor. The doctor carefully examined Spooky. Then he said, "I'm very sorry, but there is nothing I can do to help your pet. There isn't a cure for his sickness." Sherry and Mommy felt terrible. The doctor was really saying that Spooky was going to die.

"Is he going to hurt a lot?" they wanted to know. "Would it be better to put him to sleep?"

The doctor said Spooky wouldn't be in pain; so they decided to take him back home and try to keep him comfortable.

A few days later Sherry called Mommy. "Spooky is in the bathtub, and he has died." The whole family were very sad. Spooky had been their special pet for a little more than seven years, and now he was gone.

They dug a deep hole beside the wall at the back of the house where they had first found Spooky. Sherry and Mommy tenderly wrapped him and laid him in a nice box. Then they put the box into the hole and filled the hole with dirt. Daddy and Grandma felt sad, too.

Perhaps, just perhaps, in heaven Jesus will have pets waiting for us just like the precious ones we've had here. Whatever He has planned for us, we know it will be even better than anything we can dream of now. How wonderful!

Above: Daddy (Elwood), Dena, Sherry, and Mommy (Amy)

Below left: Dena and Sherry hold Pretty Boy and Darling, while Mommy teaches Boodle how to stand.

Below right: Mommy holding Pretty Boy and Darling. Darling is giving her a "kiss" while Pretty Boy looks away.

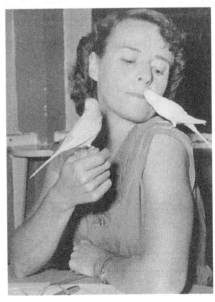

Above: Sherry (left) and Dena (right) with Boodle, Pretty Boy, and Darling.

Right: Pretty Boy (left) greets Darling (right).

Below: Darling trying to help Mommy write.

Above: Mommy, Sherry, Dena, and Daddy together with their special pets.

Left and below: Daddy, Mommy, Dena, and Sherry getting ready to go to the Philippines.

Boodle was always eager to go with the family in the car.

Amy with her mother, Mabel Hubley (age 85).
After Mabel's husband died, she joined Amy and her husband
in the Philippines.

Other Books in This Series

Little Amy was just a year and a half old when she and her mommy and daddy sailed away to India as missionaries. The little family and their fellow missionaries stood on the deck watching San Francisco grow smaller and smaller as the ship slipped out into the wide Pacific Ocean. Little Amy's parents were very thankful to be safely on that ship, for two of their family had nearly missed

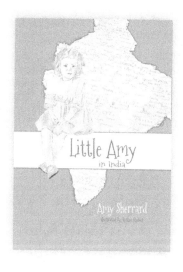

it! But that excitement was just the beginning of adventures and miracles they could not even imagine. Join Little Amy and her parents as they follow Jesus' call to "go into all the world and preach the gospel."

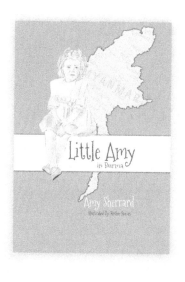

For several years, Amy and her parents had been missionaries in India. Now they were going to live and work in another place called Burma. Here they would meet a mischievous monkey, hear an angel's voice, and make more friends for Jesus. Join Little Amy and her parents as they continue their missionary adventures, following Jesus' call to "go into all the world and preach the gospel."

Other Resources by the Publisher

- Bible lessons for all ages
- Nature object lessons
- Character-building songs
- Bible learning books
- Bible games

- Scripture songs
- Posters
- Bible timeline
- VBS programs
- ++ Much more!*

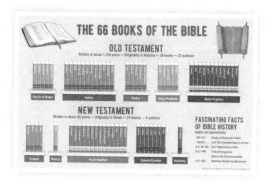

*For more information: 1-423-771-9228

sales@mybiblefirst.org • www.mybiblefirst.org

Complete, full-color catalog online